Down on the Farm
GOATS

Sally Morgan

QEB Publishing

Library of Congress Control Number: 2007000551

ISBN 978 1 59566 389 4

Written by Sally Morgan
Designed by Tara Frese
Editor Corrine Ochiltree
Picture Researcher Nic Dean
Illustrations by Chris Davidson

Publisher Steve Evans
Creative Director Zeta Davies
Senior Editor Hannah Ray

Printed and bound in China

Picture credits

Key: t = top, b = bottom, c = center,
l = left, r = right, fc = front cover

Alamy / Renee Morris 8 tr, Steve Sant 8 bl; **Arco
Images** / Tim Hill 9, 13 bl / Tim Manley 19; **Ardea** /
M.Watson title page, 22 / John Daniels 4, 12, 16 bl;
Barn Goddess Fainters / Stephanie Dicke 17 bl;
Corbis / Owen Franken 13 tl / Vander Zwalm Dan 18;
FLPA / Ariadne Van Zandbergen 5 / Sarah Rowland
7/ Nigel Cattlin 14, 15 ct / Gerard Lacz 16 tr / R.P.
Lawrence 17 tr; **Getty Images** / Siede Preis,
Photodisc Green fc / Terry Vine,Stone 15 bl;
NHPA / Daniel Heuclin 10 / Susanne Danegger 11;
Still Pictures J-L Klein & Hubert,BIOS 6.

CONTENTS

Words in **bold** can be found in the Glossary on page 22.

Goats on the farm

Did you know that goats produce milk and meat for us to eat? Goats are popular farm animals and provide people with more meat and milk than any other farmed animal.

Goats are popular farm animals in Africa.

Most goats are friendly and gentle animals. There are hundreds of millions of goats around the world. The biggest numbers are found in Asia and Africa.

Goats from nose to tail

Pygmy goats are tiny. They are about the size of a lamb. The Saanen goat from Switzerland is much larger. A fully grown Saanen goat is about 3 ft. (1 m) high at the shoulder. They can weigh up to 176 lbs. (80 kg). That's as much as four six-year-old children.

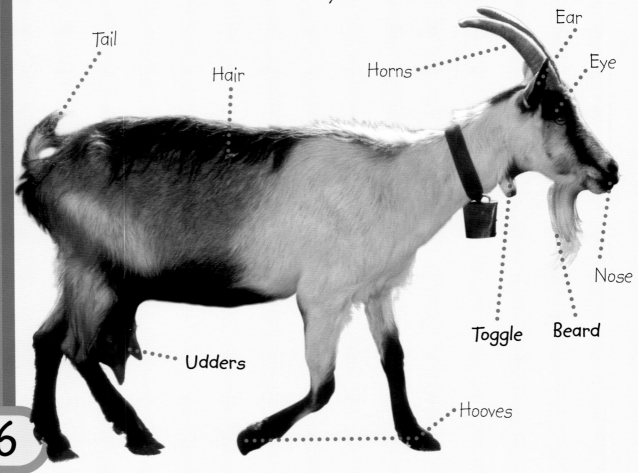

Tail

Hair

Horns

Ear

Eye

Nose

Beard

Toggle

Udders

Hooves

Almost all goats grow beards. However, the beard of a male goat, called a **billy** goat, is longer and thicker.

Height of a six-year-old child

Height of a goat

FARM FACT
The funny things dangling from the throat of many goats are called toggles. A toggle is just a piece of skin covered with hair, but nobody is sure what it is for!

It's a goat's life...

A baby goat is called a **kid** and a female goat is called a **nanny**. A baby goat grows inside its mother for five months before it is born.

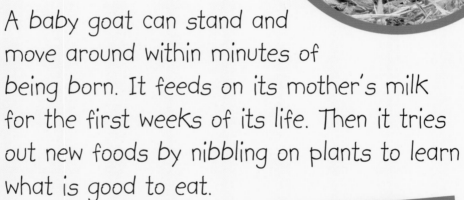

A baby goat can stand and move around within minutes of being born. It feeds on its mother's milk for the first weeks of its life. Then it tries out new foods by nibbling on plants to learn what is good to eat.

Young goats love to explore their surroundings.

After three or four months, the young goat leaves its mother. A young nanny goat is ready to have her own baby once she is about six months old. A goat lives between 12 and 16 years.

9

Greedy goats

Goats are good at escaping from their pens, especially if they spot tasty plants to eat on the other side! Many goats can jump as high as 5 ft. (1.5 m) and can crawl under fences and gates, too.

These hungry goats have climbed a tree in search of food!

Goats eat all sorts of plants. They like to eat the leaves and stems of trees and **shrubs**. Often, they stand on their back legs to reach the higher leaves. Goats also eat grass and weeds.

This goat is standing on its back legs to nibble at leaves on the branch of a tree.

FARM FACT
Goats are very nosy animals, and they like to explore. Some goats have been known to pull clothes from a clothes line. They do not eat the clothes. They just nibble them to see what they taste like!

When goats find a new plant that they haven't eaten before, they hold the plant in between their lips. That way, they can see if it tastes good before eating it.

11

Milk and meat

Many goats are kept for their milk. Nanny goats produce milk in their udders once they have given birth to a kid. They have to be milked every day. On some farms, nanny goats are milked by a machine. Goats can also be milked by hand.

This goats' cheese is being made into round shapes.

Goats' milk tastes similar to cows' milk. It can be made into yogurt and cheese.

Goats are also kept for meat. The meat from a goat is very popular in parts of Africa and the Middle East.

Curly-haired goats

Some goats are kept for their wool. The wool from Angora goats is made into a soft **yarn** called **mohair**. This is used to knit sweaters and other clothing.

Angora goats grow thick **ringlets** of wool.

Cashmere wool comes from the Kashmiri goats that live in the mountains of Asia. Cashmere is the most expensive wool in the world. The goats are combed to remove the fine hairs that lie close to their skin. This hair is made into cashmere.

14

Angora goats have to be **sheared** twice a year.

The skin of a goat can be made into leather. The leather is very soft and is often used for making gloves.

This tambourine has vellum stretched across it.

15

Gorgeous goats

PYGMY GOATS

Pygmy goats are very small. They are just 20–24 in. (50–60 cm) high at their shoulder. They have a small, rounded body. Pygmy goats are very friendly.

GOLDEN GUERNSEY

This is a small goat. It has a body that is covered in golden hair. Golden Guernsey goats produce a lot of milk, which can be made into yogurt and cheese.

16

BAGOT

The Bagot is one of the oldest breeds of goat. Bagots have been around since the 1380s. They have long horns and are covered by long, shaggy hair.

FAINTING GOATS

These goats come from North America. They are also called "stiff-legged" goats. When they are frightened or excited, the muscles in their legs freeze. They fall over and lie very stiff for a few seconds. Then they get up again!

Goats around the world

SWEDEN

The goat is a symbol of Christmas in Sweden. In the past, it was the **tradition** for a member of the family to dress up like a goat to deliver Christmas presents. Today, many Swedish families put a straw goat under their Christmas tree.

Straw goats for sale at a Christmas market.

18

KENYA

Goats are valuable animals in Kenya, in Africa and a person's wealth is often judged by the number of

goats they own. When a wedding takes place, the groom's family gives gifts to the bride and her family. A bride is usually given a goat as a wedding present.

UKRAINE

It is traditional in the Ukraine to sing carols on Christmas Eve. In the past, the carol singers were accompanied by a goat. Today, one of the singers dresses up like a goat, instead.

Goats' milk smoothie

You can drink goats' milk and also use it to make yummy smoothies.

You will need one banana, 1 lb. (500 g) of fresh, soft fruit such as strawberries or raspberries, 2 cups (500 ml) fresh goats' milk, and 4 tablespoons of honey.

1 Peel the banana and break it up into a few pieces.

2 Ask an adult to put the banana pieces and other fruit into a blender or a food processor. (Save some fruit pieces for decoration.) Blend together for a few seconds, so the fruit makes a runny mixture.

20

Warning to parents and teachers: Check that children do not have any food intolerances before carrying out the activity above.

3 Add the milk and honey to the blender or food processor. Blend until the mixture is frothy.

4 Pour the mixture into some tall glasses and scatter the extra fruit on top. Drink your smoothie right away!

5 You can make many types of smoothies by using different fruits. In summer, you could use black currants or cooked gooseberries. In autumn, you could use blackberries. For a special treat, add a scoop of vanilla ice cream to your smoothie. Delicious!

Glossary and Index

beard   hairs that grow on a goat's chin

billy   a male goat

cashmere   an expensive wool made from the hair of Kashmiri goats

kid   a baby goat

mohair   a type of wool from the Angora goat

nanny   a female goat

ringlets   hair that grows in long curls

sheared   when animal hair is removed using a special razor

shrubs   small bushes or plants

toggle   skin that hangs down underneath a goat's throat

tradition   a custom or way of doing something that is passed from parent to child

udders   the part of a female goat where milk is made

vellum   dried animal skin that people used as paper many years ago

yarn   a thread used to knit clothes or make cloth

22

Ideas for teachers and parents

- Read about different types of goats. Make factsheets about the different breeds. Find out which breeds are kept for milk and which breeds are better for meat.

- Visit a children's farm where children can see goats up close.

- Find poems or nursery rhymes about goats, such as the "Three Billy Goats Gruff." Encourage the children to write their own poems or short stories about goats.

- Buy some goats' milk and ask the children to taste it. Then, taste some cows' milk. Which do they prefer? Read the information on the carton. What does the milk contain? Why is it good for you? Find out why sick people and young children are sometimes told to drink goats' milk rather than cows' milk.

- Read about the different types of cheese that can be made from goats' milk. Find out how goats' cheese is made. Go see a cheese counter in a supermarket or a specialty cheese shop. There is a wide range of goats' cheeses on sale in supermarkets. They come in many shapes and some are covered in different herbs and spices.

- Make a collage of a goat. Take a large piece of white paper and draw the outline of a goat on it. Look through old magazines and cut out any pictures of goats and goat-related subjects. Collect scraps of material. Stick these on the outline to make a fluffy, textured goat.

- Make a wordsearch using the goat-related vocabulary in this book.

- Mohair and cashmere wool come from goats. Look for clothes made from these wools. Ask the children to touch them to feel how soft they are.

PLEASE NOTE

Check that each child does not have any food intolerances before carrying out the milk tasting activity above.